COLLECTOR OF LAPSED TIMES

col-lection, from Latin *co* + *ligere*, to gather together

col-lection, from Latin *co* + *legere*, to read with another

DAVID APPELBAUM

COLLECTOR OF LAPSED TIMES

B G S P

THE **BLACK SPRING**
PRESS GROUP

First published in 2024
An Eyewear Publishing book, The Black Spring Press Group
Maida Vale, London W9,
United Kingdom

Cover design and typeset by Edwin Smet
Cover photograph by Kate Hamilton

The right of David Appelbaum to be identified as author of
this work has been asserted in accordance with section 77
of the Copyright, Designs and Patents Act 1988

ISBN 978-1-915406-60-6

The editor has generally followed American spelling and punctuation at the author's request.

BLACKSPRINGPRESSGROUP.COM

Amanda   Harry   Steve   Deborah

David Appelbaum, founder of Codhill Press, has
worked in the university as well as in publishing.
Former editor of *Parabola Magazine*, he is the
author of *Everyday Spirits* (SUNY Press), *notes on
water* (Monkfish), and more recently, *Portuguese
Sailor Boy* (BSPG, Eyewear).

TABLE OF CONTENTS

2

I

ON BEDROCK

There is your pocket, a residuum.
Splinters of schist, rhombic, tooth-like, smooth, round flat
sucking stone (salty), a small pyramidal stone from the library
of Alexandria, amber heart stuck in the *faux* back of your mother's
jewelry case.

Stones in the side pockets of your car, inukshuk of feldspar,
petrified whale's tooth, pyrite, jasper, diorite, ballast stone
from Lord Ashburton, stone from an ancient hand axe, stone
from the barrio at Belleview, stone that blinded your right eye,
stones thrown in war by catapult (relying on tension and gravity),
through store front windows on Kristallnacht—with a debtor's note
coated in flaming tar.

Stones on shelves that once held books, marl your father culled
from Guadalcanal, granite from the oubliette at Breendonk,
chalcedony implanted in dungeon walls at _____, marble chipped from
the viaduct bombed at Gordes, bridges, abutments, crypts, catacombs;

stones the builder overlooked, cobbles, shards, stones that
fell from the sky in earth's dawn, whetstone, curling stone,
grindstone, clast, stone made to pass for a godling, skipping stones
from boyhood, stones cut and ciphered with human knowledge
before cast into the Pacific for future readers.

In the alembic, stone of the philosophers.

Quartz and aventurine, bloodstone and carnelian, green
chrysoprase, cherry stone, the stone that wasn't thrown,
gall, kidney, bladder stone—fruits of the human organ—
stone that brought the giant down, stone that blocked the cave,
stone from the road to Emmaus, spirit stone;

stones in the corners of rooms:
anchor stones, calendar stones from root cellars, stones
in the shape of apiaries, *tsovim* of all shapes and sizes,
a small slate one on your grandfather's memorial, pumice
stone to scrape off dead skin,

stone for remembrance—much for the soul
to witness—stone coins for eyes of the dead, radioactive stone
chipped from a *naga* at Osaka

stone to which your bones will calcine and whiten in utter dark.

BIRDHOUSE

In the atelier, each wall was crowded with painted birds. On one
common birds... robins, wrens in mudstone, crows in black iron
oxide from the Triassic. They streamed to a portico limed with guano
which real birds taken by the realism deposited on a stone courtyard.

Live or simulated fled the south wall where raptors were vying
for prey. Kestrels diving for salmon in bluestone oceans, kites
with beaks like cicatrices, falcons along the empyrean, serpents dangling
from their talons—withal a desire that arose in scummy tidal pools
a million years before. A cacophony of fear and feeding frenzy,
the din of fern forests bathed with volcanic thunder.

Ash on the hearth where burial had been by fire. Slobber of predation.
Spectacle sunset like a miasma settling in an acidic atmosphere. Moon like
a migratory adjunct, compass of a carnal wish for flight, leavening
solidity of the plaster columns watchful with a silent, impenitent stare.

On a wall opposite, a bestiary, a slate pterodactyl, secretion of flight a dark stain
on its breast, catechisms said of it. Over a field of terracotta, devices of
imagination, griffin, roc, simurgh, sphinx, each poised before a fatal blow,
chalk white bones of the dead. The simurgh, the largest, soars over snakes
of rivers, walled cities of worshippers whose temple roofs gleamed under the artiste's
brush, with a multiplicity of small birds struggling to keep pace. Stationary below,
a sphinx with the riddle that undid history. Rhomboid, circle, trefoil, arrow.

Overlooking the dead on the fourth wall, the most mute and reclusive,
with yellow folds of thought, were firebirds, birds of war, their destined
regeneration without finality, light skipping away into a book, thick layering
to offer a tiny tomb of the *ka*-soul several pages, enraging armies of storks,
gaps of print that feed disquiet, boredom, giddiness.

The phoenix flies from its own covering, fragments that
disperse as well as gather, a theatre in flames, hyperventilated
by the tongue reading a new section on color, the happy and
the damned in battle no longer.

Wings extended, sliding through a slit under the door, birds defined by
feathers rather than form, the fire is white, made by a great
number of small mirrors stealing words from each.
Growing and ebbing, clarity jointed with obscurity, logic with
madness, light transmits heat, the final firebird of the series singes
its comrades, charring a spongy, cavernous background, sealing
itself in a room without oxygen, alone with its self-perfection. Fire the color
of whispers, stars, heartbreak, and the indrawn breath.

This wall was a *trompe d'oeil* that hid the artiste's real creation, a phoenix
cast in solar flames.

THE CALCINE TRACE

The ocean became a source the day my bid at a county auction won a crate of seashells.
Dark ceriths, angel wings, coquinas, tritons, lucinas,
junonias, baby ears, cowries, whelks, wentletraps. A Gestalt. Each, an
empty inside pleated and sealed off from an outside, like a saint's grotto. A
chamber that whimpered an ethereal bleat, a fold that, revealing
form, became free, a commanding voice that spoke the mother tongue
as well as one foreign, as if from a necklace of whelks on the porch post,
crackling into dispute. Supper fires, oil lamps, a gale outside port holes,
breath that fell into sleep, all argued, a windowpane in a window, rooms
tucked into pockets of a raincoat hung on the rack, a bed, a night stand.

Leaving not contrary to staying, my house, the last of late, the latest cranny
for shells, was hallowed by their prattle. I left in early winter before
a pale sun amplified sounds on closely guarded roads, torture without words
behind closed doors, and to follow my summons, diverted me to fields sour with
spoilt corn, crows with mussel shells in their beaks. To lie there,
welcomed by a life unlived, seen in tidal pools that gleamed under banks of sleep,
what roused me from that hypnotic drone was a vision of a single boat heading
out of sight, where ruined ribs of a lucina blotted a gray
moon and through them a sea breeze murmuring *must not stay, must not dream,
must turn back, must wake.*

BENARAS

Your father's pipe collection, size by size, were briars except a single calabash,
a semi-circular oak rack holding a smoked glass humidor, well of complacence,
of tobacco dried in Balkan chicken coops, redolence pricking your
nostrils as a rickshaw sways past veiled women balancing muslin
bundled in plastic drop cloth on their heads, men, once child beggars intentionally
lamed at birth, limping beside oxen.

We are led by a cauldron of smells, cabbage, henna, asafetida, camphor,
always offal, odors swarming to a cloying incense that guided our
small cart through the miasma. There, an absence of fire that
would cauterize our nostrils, whence the old pipe smell, a long wood match
struck in memory against a rough brick surface in the wreath of which
a rush would rise skyward. There were names to boot, apple, billiard, bulldog,
churchwarden, Dublin, freehand, vest pocket.

In interwoven folds of sleep, hysteresis of desire, feeling would fall cold and
dead in your chest, opening a distance from the world, the claxons' blare,
bells and whistles, drivers' commands in a language nearest to prayer,
encirclements of cows, groomed, preened, and painted for fiesta. Once,
with a group of women, a young goat, trussed and carried on a birch pole,
along with bags of felt, made by fretting, not weaving, a *sadhu*, snake
emerging from a metal pipe, chanted meaningless syllables while his blank
gaze soared beyond where a horizon grounded the blue dome
over earth, beyond any claim to fidelity.

COINAGE OF MERCY

The jar of pennies would be an example, a mass as protected as a walled city,
Dubrovnik, Avila, Carcassonne...Troy, you save along with other sufferings,
of wells, cooking fires, beds, prayer rugs, amulets against the dark
crust of stars that records lives transformed, lowering north winds that
shred bracken and wild rocket, the stone beach strewn with ships,
not all the enemy's. It is as you are. The contained sustaining the contained, indefinitely,
making it able to hear a glass mouth whisper *collect yourself*, be like the
rose that husbands its scent or the monk who saves alms for the poor,
so the miscreant will know mercy.

Gather your thoughts, that they may be as under a vinculum, made
simple, guileless, that discord can agree under pearled clouds that
the storm beckons particles of light that surge past the
glass shoulder, filling the neck to the rim where forbearers of the archons
gather, a host by way of cause. There a mind has no final term
or limit, like a city irrigated with scented water, realized in
impetuosity, the sum of its inner qualities, an infinite syllable can't pronounce.
Znojmo, Harer, Mdina, Budva. In dispersion collect your will, fireflies
over meadow grass, a uniform flicker, august stars convened after a rainstorm,
euthymeme that proves absence holds its own body aloft. Each wall,
of glass, stone, wood, flesh, feeling, envelops the uncounted, even as you
feel happiness as unbearable as the void,
stones that witnessed the Templars murdered in their beds,

that mark a virtual stain on courage, on all barter and exchange
that followed, not absolved by rumors of the heart's malaise. Gather
yourself in force against betrayal, dwell in the citadel made by you for you.

It will cost dearly.

SEA CHARTS

Unrolling the map you bought me that cold winter by the Seine, the city having defused the brown shirts' ordnance, at the margins where paper, fluted in the breeze. dissolved to reality, the sea, unplumbed, linked with a name drunk sailors once gave human cargo, speckled with wind roses and rhumb lines, monsters (Typho and Hydra) that rode on Latin letters, revenants and serpents, giant heads blowing storm winds from four compass points, and the ships—barques, schooners, junks, dhows—armed against nature with a will to ply its fading cobalt surface.

You whispered *portolan* before disappearing from an abandoned cafe. I want that word back, to be freed from obsession over distance, direction, and safe anchorage, over angst since I fear water in all forms and was born so.

We might then sit at a table in another city built on gold stolen from native commissionaires and read the secret language in Salviati's map (1525). The Tierra Firme, earthen embankments encircling hallowed ground where their worship kept crown and scepter is now brown verdure, soon to be pillaged, colored red. The future unveils under the cartographer's hand, as I can show you on portolans in my collection, Gutierrez's of the Atlantic, for instance, or Truadec's. You and I can climb the hill, overrun by conquistadors, bridges patrolled for chimeras, under roofs of sky, to see what navigation has wrought with the jewels of Chichén Itzá—necklaces for wives of merchants.

The clocks silent, the baying doesn't come from dogs, the *puce* sells drowned sailors' uniforms. I wish for time to read the dynasties to you, time now shrunken, impotent change, sinuous, drawn out. The bookseller is here still, offering other portolans, this one with a mausoleum of a pillaged temple.

INSIGNIA OF WAR

The summer at Schroon Lake, men away at war. A cottage beside the
chapel in a pine grove, Russian icon whose gaze guards unmilled pews,
the riddle of a row boat beneath. You said it was for the dead, for transport
to the carrick across the water.

Envelopes came that day, thick was for bad news, onionskin for love letters,
a contact print of a Navy cruiser, some rock-strewn shoreline, three army patches.
In green light, their threads loose from salt, a rifle their call to prayer and
service, edges finished on a marrow machine, impossible to undo. They were a
singular event that drew others to it, a book bought in Osaka, a Flying Tigers
patch on page 48, a photograph of an unknown soldier, 1st Infantry, dog tags
with 516th Signal Brigade.

You folded the official note. It stayed in your pocket.
We lunched near budding loosestrife. That afternoon you rowed across the
lake, I could see you weeping.

There is a great A, red thread, the double D, 31st Division, gold talons,
17th Airborne, black hourglass, 7th Division. Apples ripen, their fragrance
lifting a storm window, the patches console us, an almost forgotten
passage from _____, I'm at the lake, rolled up jeans, calling to the other
side, touching your face wet with tears, waiting for you to tell what ended.

The next summer we climbed the ruins, my heart breaking where a
lightning strike left a mark under the collapsed altar like an infantry insignia,
a swallows' nest on top. Where the water's lip curled back in drought,
I have a meltdown. Islands have appeared, the lake looks different, I do a
sketch of the rowboat landing.

Evenings now, I look at my collection, swifts diving at us from a pocket
of eaves, the foxfire lakeside, its phantom glow within which frogs snap at
Caddisflies by a dock, a devil wind churns cattail cotton, dropping it where
pure springs disappear into earth.

LICORICE

Easter, a linden tree hung with painted eggs, sheath of wheat against
the trunk, bitter herbs, a doll with tinsel wings, monks chanting by
the bookstalls of Grona. Men drink *ratafia* at tables, *fajol* cakes, aroma
of lamb roasting with fennel. Reading a Catalan edition of *Quixote*, he buys
a tin of licorice for his throat, hands Celine a lozenge. Similarly, years after,
where ferries ply through Channel mist, Dieppe is all bells, another mass,
air heavy with pulverized cement from a condemned seawall where the
Canadian beachhead once had faltered. On a side street purpled with fallen mulberries,
a shop with netsuke, another selling philately supplies, tweezers, magnifying
glasses, cellophane envelopes, a tin of Amarelli for Celine, for rail stations,
on night trains to bribe border guards who inspect passports while the
locomotive on black rails soothes sleeping infants. Sun
slants from a storefront to the street so it is no longer possible to be unseen.

She tells him that on solstice in her village they would sing through the night,
roasting a wild boar from the forest, green turnips from the fields,
gooseberry wine, and marc. After the dance, there were gifts for everyone, sea shells,
jasmine, wild plums, and when they would fall down asleep, fierce *sangliers*
running through mist of their dreams would attack train cars of sleeping children.

He is out from the shop, she has melted into a cortège marching toward
the beach, dog tags rattle against an armful of licorice tins, leaving behind
a silver locket, an opera ticket, keys to her apartment in Marseilles, so that
he would know not to expect her return. Nonetheless he combs every backstreet,
fading yellow lamps replaced with interrogating blue-white klieg light,
harbormaster ordering the warships to block passage, there is her scarf,
under hooves of a herd of goats, along with a jasmine bouquet, mixed with black
lozenges flung across sea-damp wool, to absorb the all-penetrating dark of
his shadow. Waves lap under the pier, song deadened in a crescendo of silence.

MYCOLOGY

He drew with charcoal, it is true, on homemade wallpaper, two mushrooms
(*Amanita citrine*), after pulverizing burnt sticks from the fire, screening wet fibers,
shading image with the mind's light, though art did not interest him. The charcoal
sketch was allerium in which spores became stipe and cap, adding a mark of eternity to
his specimen collection. On the floor, a silver samovar kept hot tea, a kiln made from
a steel barrel, burlap stapled into sacks, and piles of fungi, foraged from memory, that
emitted a smell when crushed like burning leather.

The drawing is shaped like the whirr of cicadas in July heat, its taste the sweet almond
of cyanide, its feel on the palm, blister of ice, its sign, illegible. The
specimens, a passion, are not assembled, *Boletus* and *Lactarius*,
in piles, *Russula* its flightiness musty beside the staid *Psalliola*. The collection begins in
Dubrovnik, by the city walls, the original, a *Boletus*, now looks like a
shrunken humanoid head.

The table, his father's sea chest, had a porcelain statue, its
derisive smile beside two ivory netsuke rested beside an icon of St. Anthony
(copied by Sandra), a book on the afterlife, with the proposition that
survival is a measure of value. The samovar would be
witness to a photo he found in the priest's barn,
proof, it seemed, as did another icon in a consignment shop spared from
devastation, the image of a statue behind the church, decapitated but otherwise
intact, saved in a flood that buoyed it, pleading like a
supplicant door to door as it floated down the street, in memory of the golden gills of
Psylocibe cubensis, a vitrine filled with charcoal sketches that
replicated furrows of the brain, along with tusks of an African elephant,
a library notice for overdue books, a crucible of ashes left from burning his
passport photo as well as those of a family album, where the contingency of
birth on faces he knew, lit by chance imaginings, passed through
glass and above, lit by a radiance from those who had
touched him with their quiet intending, and then, forgotten under brown
dust, coating the book—all in a mirror holding the image of St. Anthony,
impassionate.

NABOKOV'S DREAM

We slept cliffside on nights without fog, under noctilucent clouds.
A ferry horn near midnight, few arriving from the mainland, fishing boats in search of
cod, oil lamps on deck, a wake of twinned wave caps. That day, the yoga
teacher gave me a butterfly, first of my collection, a Painted lady (*Rhopalocera*)
found near the lighthouse. She said it mimicked the *ahamkara* so that for once in life I
might see myself, really. At the lookout we lunched, osprey dove for herring,
thistle froth rode out a sea breeze, dragonflies harrowed the hillside, millers on
yarrow, you pull me downhill to a building named Swallowtail, our
sprint through colonies of Monarchs, disassembling, realigning behind our gasping for air.

Swirl, loft, spin, hover, tilt, each body exuding a material world from its depths,
without 'pathos of distance,' a concatenation of postures in the play of
existence, that raised a fine powder in front of our eyes. *Don't go back to
sleep*, you said, gather the sealed-off pages now torn, wings
pinioned, remember gold pollen hidden in nectar that draws wisdom to it so
that the light keeper will recognize you.

On the island (there were many), you would point to specimens in the
gorse, Angel-wing, Hairstreak, Sulphur, a sensed presence still enough
for capture. In that concentration, a collection grew as dust becomes patience,
wish enfolds act, choice invites destiny. Phosphorescent waves litter
the sand with periwinkles as we hunt night-flying *Lunas*, you said their
single day was like ours, filled with desire for desire, enduring stress of a
thousand 'little springs', a disquiet of joy. When the pendulum moves, the
wings take flight. No fear of falling as you glide along
dreamlines, invisible, sure, immovable. Attached to nothing, in certainty of
stars filtered through fog, a leaping that exhausts happiness within that
space exhumed by light, by photons' conscious intent, empty of all but
chance, in dark of light.

Abandon your faith, she said, in the urgency of being real, the surrender
that accomplishes each loss.

THE MISSING KEY

Dust collects under the door.
You would go in, a bronze key between your fingers, one of a collection,
bow, shaft, collar, pin—words fit together but 'turn' is forbidden. Sops for the dog,
blood for the guardians, *baruchas* for the enablers. There are other doors
but without keyholes. The only window shows you a pegboard on which
missing keys have numbers, no names, iron, steel, ivory, rare and antique,
recalling narrow cobbled lanes, coal merchants stammering at day's start, live
rooster in the window box, to be slaughtered for *shabbat*. Someone selling
warbonds would knock, a census taker, an insurance agent, all without avail.
No one was home.

You want to ask, why can't they read, he is dead, my father is in another town,
locked behind another door, feeding those with him the bread from his mouth.
He is at the shore, raking salt, a gun, a secret letter written by his
captain, suing for peace. Hear, O nations, words used over and again, grown
blunt to bludgeon our ears, no one answers the untended door, bodies laid out
for a morgue, around each neck, a wood key, to let in, to be let out, to read
the script, ascertain the cause, take a proper course of action. For illiterate
angels of death.

With a tumbler of schnapps, you would read each a few symbols done in a
child's hand, birthmark of a life's destiny, stopping at one as if
struck by a resemblance to your father's face, of when he climbed the
barbed wire to free the prisoners locked within. He will take your
hand, *tefillin* wrapping mangled fingers, to a room that no longer
exists, whose echoes are absorbed by velvet curtains, in a voice clear and
low, would say which key holds promise, which is blessed or cursed—before sound
blends to an inaudible hum in your ear, a pulse maddened by the handcuffs
at his wrist.

MOTHER'S DAY

Weight of glass, petals pressed to a translucent skin, their veins a
map, glue overlay with thumbprint as if phloem still pulsed, as if its vessel still
awaited joy's outcome. Tape the edge when you're told. *Do as you're spoken to,*
words repeat years after the present given, paid for, put in your collection
as shard and broom dust, a remainder more painful than injury
inadvertently inflicted, remixed with similars, your voice out of a stranger's mouth.
You expected praise for time lived, for notes that ought to have been
written instead of impressions of flowers between wax paper, a cardboard carton serving
to file splotches of gray-green, fragrance diluted, fixed in a wooden frame. Yet like
the glass petals, life drained from her face, a mask preened in wait for the War
Department telegram, joyful tears douse a cigarette, an ocean windrose and a
landing boat that carried him, a name that escaped her mouth, landed on
salt sand gored by ten thousand boot heels.

Dear mother, I have sought permanence silently pressing together two squares of glass,
to create a forgiving in which only an afterlife remains. In that handbook,
hope comes after fear as fruit from flower. But with your ovary barren, a story
comes to no end, entries empty on blank archival paper, labels torn or absent, assembled
by an inattentive soul. Their home in the heart, an infinity of sand, carnage
from an assault, endless and endlessly made, is barren of
purpose like the casing of a seed perpetually under glass. It listens for the soughing of a
final syllable, just as salt on a sea breeze tastes of your dead lips.

FIXTURES

My grandfather built a house for us. He was a plumber from Krakow who died in a pump room, installing a valve. The ghost never left. Toilets ran, faucets dripped, fittings leaked, steam spoke from radiators.

My father came home in dress uniform. I cried when a strange man tried to hold me.

The concrete foundation had a crack. The basement housed sea creatures.

A lawn-to-be was planted in rye. In a single day, from dawn to dusk, he turned sod over with a pitchfork. When it grew in, grass was mixed with plantain, which I had to weed after school.

Of the war he never spoke. Names he never mentioned: Midway, Guadalcanal, Tarawa, the Coral Sea. Every Monday evening, in parade dress, he drove to Stamford to an Army meeting.

I found the Rising Sun, a Japanese flag, torn, riddled with bullet holes, wrapped around a bayonet. I thought it was grandfather's.

He was the reason the sheep broke out of their pen, wire fence tufted with wool, to graze roadside first, then in Victory gardens of neighbors. Later it was the same with the pet sow.

My father played chess with me every night for a year. Tears of shame reddening my cheeks, I cried when I lost. In our last game, I won on a knight's gambit. We never played again.

I hid in the coal bin where I would play games with my grandfather's ghost. There were chess sets made from scraps of paper labeled 'pawn' et cetera, toy soldiers, kitchen utensils, clinkers. Soon I was a collector of books on chess. Kotov, Nimzowitsch, Bobby Fischer.

My grandfather's sister, Tante Faiga, died in the Old World, working on
Kindertransport. She seemed to live in the mudroom outside the kitchen,
from where smells of mushroom barley soup mixed with the bleating
of sheep.

Although no one ever found me, she would bring olive loaf sandwiches
to the back of the bin, whose darkness was denser than a tomb,
dark as when the windows steamed over from our tears.

The house was quietest when the evening brought him with a Scotch and local
news in the *Norwalk Hour*.

GARBAGE COLLECTION

From a hilltop the feather collection mimicked an island. It was woven together by tides reweaving skeins' fiber, plastic bags, motor oil cans, candy wrappers, paper diapers, and charred wood, effluvia of a thousand civilizations.

Gulls swooped, silent until a short shriek, a flourish upwards, then guano dropped onto it.

Fishing charts had it marked 'danger,' its invisible tendrils reaching to foul engine propellers. Feather Island, as it was called, was in the red zone.

Village children row the short distance to pilfer soda cans for school projects. Harbor porpoises (*Phocoena phocoena*), guardians of riff-raff, speak in a language of clicks, which are mistaken for insects on shore.

The island barely moves, as though tethered by sea kelp to the bottom. Winter draws it closer to land as ice shrinks water distance.

One frigid day, we watched someone walk the narrow isthmus to a mound, retrieve a tire, and roll it back with a stick. Someone else later fell in and froze to death.

There was a whale, a humpback, that grazed near it. Around the massive jaw, eyes limpid with the suffering ocean, a clenched fist of lobster tackle, ropes, metal cage, bait box, that it would wear its lifetime, like a camp prisoner.

Herring schools steered clear of its cool underbelly, even in late summer heat, as if white pellets of Styrofoam or shiny metal rings did not tempt, the way cut-up baitfish did in the trap. Soon the catch would be insufficient for the smoking shacks and the industry would have to relocate.

A gang of sea otters once unraveled a fringe of the island. Bottles, plastic bags, gasoline cans set out to form a new archipelago, but restless tides soon rounded up the stuff that had been used up, dispossessed, discarded, and remade it into Feather Island.

Over drinks, villagers debated the phenomenon. It was a garbage dump, a sign of divine largess, a den for ghosts of the Ashburton sinking. It had been there always. No, it appeared after a gale. Once winds lofted it over the marina, swamping fishing boats in dry dock. For a day the village was a tide-water dumping ground. The sea receded, the debris with it, and it was back to becoming an island.

In the village, the fox screamed in loneliness for its mate. People fed it in the arroyo to keep the chicken coops safe. It was known to swim to Feather Island in its despair and feast on gulls and puffins.

SAIGON

An intuition takes hold, now you are gone, you who have no
name you can give, who whispers half-thoughts in my ear you do not
finish. *Are you writing?* Taking hold of the pen, I don't remember
who asks the question.

The glossy match book from a collection reflects your face. I see
in you the tranquility of a child, sun drapes your skin,
cicadas in ivy, a bench by the river that flows in a quiet mind.
From the Old Quarter, the Temple of Literature, stone turtles
by the Wall of Heavenly Clarity, you made a wish before consigning
the poem to water. *In hell, smell is a talisman.*

From a single match in the book to a burning city, chemical fire, fire
of hell, infernal fire 'does not singe a sleeve.' Soldiers from the
jungle hose the slow river onto flames. Water cannot extinguish
pain. Persistence of smoke occludes remembrance, souls lose way in
the maze of solitude. The conflagration is by choice.

I see you down a *h'em* as in an allegory, hole-in-the-wall restaurants,
drinking tea at the end of which, we visit the Cu Chi tunnels, refuge from
bombs, fanning for miles under the countryside. Fragrance of vetiver. There you mixed
with ghosts—indigenous invaders—and became one yourself, a
gauzy streak of camouflage paint on an old weapons cache. On
one wall was painted PLAF.

Your sister came to hunt for you. She hadn't heard of your
poems. Visiting the French Basilica, she lit a candle using one of your
match books and disappeared into the river. *For souls who
sleep without any rest.*

In the spring, I went with you to the War Remnants Museum.
We saw the 'tiger cages' and an exhibit on Agent Orange,

which we rubbed onto your skin. It was the way I knew you
were no longer alive. At the ordnance display, you said *We
know not why bombs kill.*

Everything is rebuilt here. By faith, creation follows
destruction, bright storefronts, tourists in blue jeans, jasmine
along the river bank, a fetid miasma only in dusk of
monsoons. Infernal smell a millennia of rain will not
dissolve and not come close. I sat with coffee on a bench,
stray dogs patrol for handouts, I count phantoms
who crowd the *he'm*, not caring the living see them, inhaling
smoke from Gauloises that darkens their translucent bodies.
The dead, having no knowledge of contingency, believe they
are alive.

THE GUIDE

In mornings, the sky is red, Independence Palace is green,
tinting the earth, the river is sere, a vestigial organ,
an arterial passage now on verge of closure. Before you
came to me, to awaken, you were here with the unborn,
in a temple of the wooden Buddha holding a flower. As to
his reluctance to enter samsara, you spoke of the taste of
bread when you're hungry. *Life will call softly, without
disdain*.

I clear myself of traces since you appear only as
surprise. You know only the unexpected since without
desire, there is nothing else for choice. The river too has
forgotten the skiffs, canoes, and rowboats that assailed steel
warships, and has given over to tourist launches. Oblivion
too has a history that predates the city.

It forgets how fire burns. How near we are to wariness,
in striking a match. Physics has a short reflex time.
Blink of an eye.

FOR CROSSING

At the dock, the boat keeper holds a bag of coins. It is
made of ostrich hide, a gift from his grandmother. He wears
a coat of glass. The coins are saved for the dead as well
as the catatonic, the drowsy, the sleeping, the numb.
As he read in Homer, all must pay for passage.

The coins come from worlds apart, Etruscan, Hittite,
Sumerian, Babylonian. Some are round as a vowel,
some are notched for measure, some have a hole like
an aspirant, most are stamped with holy signs. Transport
is difficult. The boat keeper must jiggle the coins to keep
on course as the deck is piled with tea and textiles.
Ghosts of sailors vie for them, threatening to run the
boat aground. Even the deaf understand the music. Even
the bathers still on shore. It is possible to travel great
distances and hear the wind's warning, not knowing from
where it comes.

The dead are seated on Styrofoam benches, all face
seaward. Behind, smoke rises from barrel stoves, women
with wooden spoons stir pots. They know the last
glimpse is unbounded. Children play with the ferry's cat
while they sit at the bottom of a well, empty except for
pure light, and listen to faint chimes. The dry dock is arranged
like a graveyard, the many gangplanks lead to a stone
stairway but are at different distances from the town.
On the bay, many boats ply the waves but all except the
boat keeper's stay in sight of land. They fish, explore,
take pleasure behind curtained ports and return before
sundown.

From the blue sea, where dreaming begins, wind in the
keeper's coat of a sail, the boat presses on. Eventually
you will be known. We all will be known, the keeper
says, as he pours a libation from a goatskin jug. Bhikkhus wave
a censer, chanting words of reveille which rise with smoke,
two thin streams ascending, unbroken to the angelic sky.
Others pray, eyes forward since it is easy to miss the
country of their destination, it rises and sinks like flames
on damp wood, like a voice hoarse from calling.

MUSIC MAKING

In the music maker's house, there was music made by no one. It
first played 'Eine Kleine Nachtmusik' from a lacquered box, a
photo of a movie star inside the lid. Its handle lent to over-
winding. At a shop in Berlin, he bought a second-hand one
that broke after a few measures of a Bach fugue. The tinny
sound, music for one, pleased him, tears falling on metal, clapper
on a glass bell, straw against a ceramic cup. It was the
sound of vacancy. It had no echo.

There were other shops, Vienna, Madrid, Carlsbad, an
urge to collect that gave way to making. The shop held plaintive
melodies that lingered over remnants, cardboard, wood,
discarded mechanisms, flecks of paint. Passersby would stop,
to make sure they had heard something rather than nothing.
Once escaped, music rushed the ear of heaven as if to a
vacuum. Bells chiming in vaults of bones in catacombs. Dead air
embalmed with aromatic froth, as if played for seraphim.

On the walls were sketches of designs, on shelves, the
products, in wood, ivory, bone, heavy paper. It was
difficult to see which from which, pencil marks of
ordinary life coded into ingenious things, wind material-
ized into whirling lines. No one knew whether it made
a difference once the handle was cranked. One could
imagine music coming from a still-beating heart that the
music maker placed in a box, pumping like a calliope.
The sounds had magnetism and collected listeners in their
seam.

It is the last box the maker is finishing. The music is to
be perfectly pitched silence. Taking it to a window, it is Aeolian,
he lets go the crank. It plays in a register that will

never play again, its notes swallowed by no one else.
The light changes, shadows lengthen to leaves-taking,
a melody just begun undoes itself as sounds are redacted,
numbed, suppressed. Inside the box is a living space. It is
kept in a hard shell. In vertigo, it is like an 'enraged
charioteer's whiplash.' Hold it to your ear. There is
everything to learn. It is what the Sphinx said.

TREE OF YEARNING

There is nothing holy on the island. Wrapped in mediocrity
it is moored midway in a shallow bay where ships run
aground and are wrecked. That doesn't stop blessing after
blessing to be tied to a tree, beside paddocks of thyme. Its boughs watch
sky flatten under glass, bones bleached by the sea while
others pray in the cauldron of misgivings, salt
tears their remainder. It recollects the lap of seawater
against a birch bark canoe as the first people came for
mussels and berries. Then the intermittent wood ships
with cows and roosters, the luff of sail. Then the steel ferry,
diesel staining its wake, for the sake that no one will be exiled
even if in storm. The tree can't read words, the phloem feels what
they express in their serif. Wrapped in a shawl of mist,
it is a sadhu whose vigil practices austerities on earth, as
it is in heaven.

The sentry post is slave to the fierce winds of island
life. Scraps, paper, papyrus, parchment, follow ebb tides
outward, to a steel-gray ocean. They scatter, dissolve,
a fitful rain over skeletons of ships, onto spillage that trails
along the sea floor, into its caves. As if words lost to saline
still inflected dark thoughts of the drowned. As
if signal fires, lit by women anxious for hope, would
be seen those fathoms below. After a gale, the tree would
receive a new host, flutter of the heart as fingers fastened
a plea for God's favor, that the petition from someone washed
of sin linger, on behalf of souls who could no longer
remember. Silhouetted at twilight the tree huddles under
bombardment of a million stars.

The island wanders on a sea of many colors. Like a dervish
coat, like Joseph's, it has a patch for each suffering, each act

of human neglect. The froth of waves, lifted sunward, is
remnant, remembrance laps gently against the hull, is gone. It isn't
caught in the net fishermen set for pollack, though
the salt cod (*bacalao*) that Portuguese adventurers sought
keeps the taste.

When it is feast day and bells on the Anglican church call boats home,
there is nothing to keep us there. Oat cakes
and barley soup will be hot, the rooster slaughtered.
Amid laughter, the tree receives its investiture, permitting
others unaware of their own lack of feeling to voice compassion.
The vineyard at harvest will not detain the rafts that carry
us to visit the sepulcher. Shush, let us go.

HERO

I think of you in the marsh, a mud-rimmed walker being pushed past
rock moored in the icy element. You could
float. You could tread water, a body that is no longer
aware of flotation drills but like a corpse, responds to
no command, an emulsion that won't blend with saline.

I was cradling your head, overlarge in your illness,
rubbing lineament onto your neck. There was a scarf around it,
to ward off the cold. You, telling stories, recited a poem
by Yeats, a country of no destination where we each find
ourselves a ghost in a life once lived, now in eternal return.
To use a paint brush was an art of that ghost, yet you re-
counted how in the war your father discovered
masterpieces the Germans had stolen and hid.

Effervescent heroism, you called it. you would have gone
on with history and liturgy, one hour more with Celestine,
white wine from the Alsace, another transcontinental bus
ride on acid, the obit your brother wrote for Kesey. There
was a call, you fell to your knees, listening while
a subway passed through sheet metal, stopped on its
way to Berlin. You said it was a tic, a nervous jolt
through a dilemma, writer's block, then, a stroke of God.

In the aftermath, sedation was a closet out of which anger
cast you, lost to words as they moved farther
away. Slurs are curved lines that spread across many notes,
a pedal to run tones together: how you then spoke, mouth of
a hollow statue, man inside. It was the cry of a head
severed from the torso, a brain in a vat.

In stone caves beside a fresh water lake by the sea, the hiss of
bats under attack reminds me of a voice throttled. Before
betrayal it would recite uncut pages of a dream, now it and
its muse have turned ears from each other. In one version
of the poem you read, the boat survived when the captain
took the helm. It was a war poem that men leaving their
lives were given as a late benediction. Tears like water
in a holy stoup gather and become spirit as the salt residue
brings peace.

You, head abnormally large, set on stooped shoulders, pro-
gress toward the sea as villagers pass you by, seeking a word
of your tranquility. You can only genuflect. You are mute.

GLASS DIGGER

You stayed with him the last dig, Erika, for a fact. Frost
had already stippled the apple tree, a gibbous moon hung over
gulls laying claim to the garbage pit. He was
there for his bottle collection, you were 'the eye.' They
brought cash in the city which made scavenging chancy
since the hoodlums were waiting in ambush.

You feel his nerves as heavy loam falls off the
pickax, rats shriek at the encroachment, a click of
metal on crystal. The first 'mine' had been bricks, the
earthen mound by the ferry, his friend's whiskey mouth divulging
enemy secrets as wild swans flew overhead. In the
kitchen of his childhood, a cache of half-torn books—Anna
Karenina among them—gave a false sense of familiarity.
The future would be a constant. The next visit found them buried in
ashes, sown with Roman salt. Barren soil for learning.

Glass was a cash commodity in the scarcity of war. It was not
wealthy burgermeister on the black market but purveyors
of bombs who bought the contraband. Soldiers in the
wasteland had him dubbed the beer bottle thief. They blew off his
left hand. Rather than wait to be killed at dusk, he left a
mine, a small, homemade volcano.

That evening the two of you at the café were drinking
grappa. Blue smoke from the factory explosion upland,
a settling of wind in marsh grass. *If they capture you, talk.*
You had bought antibiotics and dressing. *Tell what they
want. Just do it.*

The wine sac had a tear in it. Dark fluid ran out in the
moonlight. Not wetting the table, it flashed to the earth

like quicksilver, like nitroglycerin. You had crossed your
arms over your chest, a young girl pleading with the talons
of cherubim. You would have intercepted the single eye
of the Gorgons to change his mind.

The interrogation room reassembled in the crypt of night,
the leader crowed with mock words. *The truth!* Your ears heard
only dull repetition. *Truth. Truth. Truth.*

CHANTEUSE

That summer on the Costa Brava, we stopped at a local
bazaar, a metal tray with postcards, papers curled,
images faded into gloss. In one a woman looked from some
singers into the camera's eye, a faint smile
that would trigger memory. The back was in old
German script, partially blotted. After browsing, I bought
several. It was the way my collection began.

Unknown buildings, statues, viewscapes, street fiestas:
gathering was a haphazard thing. During time, a book stall or
bric-a-brac shop would call for a stop. It was when
patriotic agitprop—Europe was in ruins—was in vogue and
I was not interested. One day in Prague, a thousand miles
away, the same postcard, the smile, and stamped over the
photo, *Judenfrau Sangerinnen*. In the album, I press
forget-me-nots alongside it. That night, the swallows that dove
at us were in a dream. Narrow dark alleys, Dutch half-doors
open, a smell of pickling fish from buildings in a
perpetuity of stone. A prolonged quiet to tell of birth and death,
the pell-mell of gunfire along side of the titter of birds
descended from above.

It was our last day. You had said it wasn't prudent to go.
Outside the Judisches Museum, chestnut was in bloom,
cloying fragrance blending with cathedral bells. There were many
things of light, bees among the chrysanthemums, butter-
flies, garlic from a kitchen. I wasn't reticent. Inside were
exhibits with small white plaques set in typescript, and
from an adjoining room, a recording of a shofar. I stood in
front of photos of the Kindertransport.

Every platform had children in lines, suitcases of card-
board fixed with twine, blankets and dolls in arms,
train windows with infants swaddled together for warmth.
Behind a silence of the moment past, black smoke of
the engine, cries of uprooted and dispossessed souls,
death in life, small unction on hope. *Don't look,* you
said, but I'd seen the gaze of her who looked everywhere
and nowhere, possessing the scene like a gargoyle at night.

An empty urn my mother kept of her dead sister, the
still-there of an anguished life. In the hour-then before
the last sentence rose with a piano's sorrow, before
the star rose for morning redemption, you whispered,
when the war ended, and heard the lie. Underground, a
subway rumbled away, deafening words that would remember
who uttered them, and why.

UNCLE MOSES

Valises sprawled under a pendant night. He would
sit cross-legged on one to barter over mint tea.

In burlap bags, henna, asafetida, fenugreek, cumin, mustard
seed, beloved of the Buddha.

The lilt of an oud played in a minor key, of a melody
that wasn't there.

With patience of shadow, he would wait, wrist-
watches, silk nylons, crystal glass, gold frame eyeglasses,
last, the silverware.

And he, as then he was, an age he would never be
(phantom years), would whisper a number that hung in
air like incense, like a death-wish.

It was for a silver coffee spoon, spoon of bone, horn,
or ivory, sugar spoon, five o'clock spoon. For a spoon from
the Lusitania.

A valise left in Strasbourg, a hotel that stole his papers,
a gym bag near Innsbruck, salt sand from Carthage.

Spoons would arrive in strange packets, with postage
in rainbow colors. They were meant for you,

He had no use for them any more than for the stars
that orbited mercifully the last night, that would never
speak of disappearance of their faithful witness.

At flea markets that you passionately visit, he would be there, a man in the room they white-washed with milk, a quizzical smile that asked whether you were being cheated, or not.

2

IN ALEXANDRIA

This is for when you get lost, she said. It was a book-
mark from a store in Maastricht. On the back she wrote
Find me. We drank sweet black tea in Alexandria. You read
from your notebook. A plaque where the great library
once stood, blue taxi cabs under a fading azure sky,
air exploding with bicycle chains and barking dogs. I
marked the Sappho book with ink, the poem about a
purple ribbon as we followed a channel etched in the
delta, under date palms along a jetty by the arsenal,
all the way to Pharos, along the Hepta stadion, ten
thousand lanterns adrift, a flotilla. In the morning
you caught a freighter to Mykonos, where the whiteness
would blind you.

There had been the terror of the Libyan desert, driving in
caravan by night without headlights—to avoid the
daytime heat. Sleep flitted with dreams that dissolved
in acid, the quarter moon made a low hissing sound.
Checkpoints where soldiers perpetually at war
would stare dumbly at passports. Sharp words screaming
in our ears with cries of ten thousand martyrs.
Toward three a.m., ruins of a Roman outpost,
bones of a saint lying in a collapsed crypt, an
aerosol of sand fleas in your flashlight beam. You
had whispered something about the Lorelei and
their inhuman love, lives without a day not given
to others, to draw the song from them.

I left for the south, the Valley of Kings, we passed
silence back and forth through forays of dragonflies. *Find me*,
you had said. There are other bookmarks to prove
the truth, one in a French edition of Napoleon's travels in
Egypt.

The cool breeze of the funeral chamber surprises
us more than the assault of hieroglyphics. I hadn't
thought death was so antiseptic.

It was odd but I spoke over a water urn with Greek
students whose hometown you would visit, young
men who still prayed for an afterlife, as their grand-
parents had. That their bones would be clean as
their flesh when lifted to heaven. On the road into
Luxor, while the driver spoke to us, the bus ran
over a water buffalo, beloved of the Akkadians.
People gathered as if for a fallen martyr.

The Egyptian word for purity means
impermanence.

Reeds were set ablaze on the way to the sea. Clouds
of smoke fumigate the souls of travelers. Xenophon
fleeing Darius in koine spoke lovingly of his enemies.
I feared missing the tramp steamer.

In an antique store, a child walked toward me with
a tray of old bookmarks. Hair, like yours, the color
of straw. *Find me.*

In Venice, at the hotel, a telegram was waiting. The
terrorist attack in the harbor, you and a pregnant girl.
You are everywhere, a *ka*-bird flying through clouds
of ether, nowhere if not above this planet.

THE GIFT

On a small silver mirror, he had written, *don't be afraid
to look*. It was a birthday gift of a spring day that chased
thoughts of cold delirium. Heft of a book,
oval of a face. You held it up after news of his
accident on the Jungfrau and saw his invisible grip.
When it had let fall the piton.

Only a thousand of us left, you thought. You take a
tram beyond a stop where it is possible to get off. A
woman you didn't know follows you. At the Rheinfall,
you throw acacia blossoms that the spew devoured. The
famous rainbow is there, promising. Downstream a
body floats face down. In a still eddy, your smile above
a school of silver koi. A fisherman shows you
the optical illusion, marsh grass packed around an old
tarp, a bucket for a head. You look again and again,
laughing because the mirage doesn't vanish.

In Schaffhausen, in a brockhaus, a second-hand mirror,
glass in pewter. The face, a crone's, stared without
recognition as she watched at the revolving door while
you visited your father's old office, where his *neshama*
said that *kugel* would be waiting for your dinner.
A visit to the medical museum, its vitrines of
monsters and grotesques, witness to divine mis-
anthropy, then to the apartment for which the attorney
had given directions. He had left his Hölderlin books
to you, in one, underlined, the words, 'our fate to have
no place to rest.' Under the eaves where Joyce had
lived, tiny birds whose voice was too quick to translate.

You follow the families, each with its own quiet
entitlement, to the lake. A man without legs begs,
you search for change, and when there is none, hand
him your silver earrings, miniature mirrors. One
palm on his heart, he prostrates himself, not rising
until you have gone. At water's edge, swans retreat
to mid-stream, disturbed by your anxieties.

On the other side, street lamps are being lit, a make-
believe city, patrolled by soldiers in starched khaki.
Above, a light throb of wings brushes the sky.
In your solitude, the moon is a glass, its face etched from
tears of those who ask to be remembered. There is
fear as you look. While on earth, you know
you will always be able to look a second time.

SEPIA

May your ink never run dry. The first specimen, a glass well under
a pewter lid, said that. Outdated as a Baedeker, it kept an
eye on the pretext of words, not betraying the voice
that spoke. A commodity all the same, like whale oil
or chamber pots, that belonged to a different saint, when
death was less capricious. You never wrote with a quill, in
defiance of your collection of inkwells. Silver, horn, or ivory
basins whose function was to hold ink, into whose dark
gaze hours of your entrancement would pass. It was
how thought dissolved in words, as if
undone by fact, that brought him back from the wordless
rim of forgetting.

On that day you typed a letter, your room by the church
was sunlit, acolytes chanted in single-file on stone scraped
by heels of a thousand masses. Swallows dove from mud
nests in the belfry, mulberry staining benches meant
for prayer. Inside, relics said to be of Saint Anthony. Poppies in
the yard, tossed roughly in wind, ones dry-pressed
under the ink well. It was to warn of surveillance that your
garret was safe no longer for meeting under lamplight,
even when the flock of bells could shush our whispers.
He would have to adapt to the poverty of the nameless
where it enters the labyrinth, words left said without voice, his
body without your warmth. It was a life sentence. You
knew he was already dead.

He had asked for a better life, not for himself. The man
in front of you holding a gun. He had walked from
twilight of that confinement into a sentry box of the solitary.
His mother took her life. Still, he would not leave underground to
appear for himself. Death is just that *zweifalt*, he once

said. Now he wanders in between the dome of stars and
this concave vault of earth, not suffering the intricacy of
waking life. The berme was raised for pilgrims like him,
for whom no trace will be left, who ask what is to be done?

The well brims. Its eye is less guarded than your
words. The monks have finished Compline. Silence
save for wolves howling from the hill top. The living are
oblivious to themselves, the dead do not know goodness.
Words would speak the complicity in each. What is left
you but to wander in pity between.

COURIER OF NEWS

The letter knife was balsa wood, as in a kit to make
toy gliders, now under heavily lacquered paint. You knew
the blade was only a function, the rest is figure and metaphor.
There were two to start the collection, both vultures poised
for road kill on jet-black phone poles. Pointed tips in a vase
with fireweed and goldenrod, warmth seeming to escape
like a solar radiance, they were glowing joss sticks. Both
were herald to news of your mission when there was
none, I put them aside in favor of using a rusty penknife,
better to rip open envelops stamped 'government business.'

It is as though I could write now with one, your words speak
from barren nib, sounding the way *Ooo* sounded as you
would lower your heavy body into a warm tub. Involuntary
joy, you said, the only kind. You were courier, news had to
get into the prison where they kept him, an oubliette with a
roofless chapel, shrines as interrogation booths. Between
the mountains where phantom giant *Luna* moths were ready
to clap your ears into deafness and amnesia, where pits
stood open for skulls to whiten along hidden stairwells. For
a talisman, I imagine, you took a wood bird, to hold in front
of you, bold as a sword, as if evil would see the sign and let pass.
Caddisflies swarmed above underbrush slashed
by your machete, as you disappeared past a rusted truck,
swans raged in fury and circled.

Stone piled on stone capping stone, a rough cairn to respect
where pilgrims ceaselessly cross. In winter a monument to the
obloquy of the world. To dig beneath in the hardpan is to
find nothing. The last trace is yet more sensible, a cicatrix
over the sun as it set that night, without remainder. Dust and
wings, signifying your becoming a bird—a raptor—in the ambush, wings

outstretched, lofting above machine guns, over the detritus
of the village like a light wooden plane gliding over a field
of chicory and poppy, swooping past hummingbirds, your
soul freed to be risen on heat currents, welcomed by the
yet-blue clouds.

DUTCH DETOUR

Number 32 in his collection had the old Gothic keyboard.
Der weg ist Offen, words when read, had sent the German convoy away
from the city to the Danish border. He preferred the sound effects of
his typewriters, dozens of all makes, to the grinding retreat of tank
treads on tarmac. You who delivered the message know the truth,
a city no longer under siege, surrounded by potato and barley fields, its cathedral
bells now free to ring in the Sabbath. No one there now
remembers how a single font saved a hundred lives
from the camps or from the pain of feeding boiled tulip bulbs to your
children, too hungry to sleep. Along one canal
is a hotel named for the battle, famous for its bar. In green fields
outside, buildings stand on stilts erected against flooding,
an order to rend the dikes that never came. You
would have crossed over the waters, with gills breathing the sea, its
unquenchable salt, death to soil whose life took millennia
to inspire.

It is true that Maastricht was under siege, and Utrecht,
armored trucks with loud speakers blasting propaganda.
You had helped lay the fuses that were never ignited, and
by night with a flashlight and a blessing from the avenging
angel, were antagonized by deaths of the first born. *Kapitulation!*
Leaflets raining from the clouds. The rage with which
you fed them to fires that men burned at dark in steel drums
in the square. Soldiers swilled from bottles, silently drunk.
A child we pulled from the river, weighted with copper
mortar shells, rucksack tangled in reeds. A single match
was needed, an incendiary spark that never came. An imprudent
wish, feckless.

He said you were expendable, a canary. You were sent to
Amsterdam, or volunteered, a rubber boat slithering along
the canals of your boyhood, your kit, candles, and nothing
else, by instinct skirting bodies, face down, heels like empty
eye sockets staring at the moon. We knew there would be
no one left to warn you. At the house of typewriters, he
said you were a writer, you wrote about heroes. I am not
a hero but if we love similarly what words name, then
'let us be watchful and sober' in this time for heroism.
I will find the village of your birth and leave your papers
at the library, that your people may read them lest the
world end in silence.

SEA GLASS

He did not find any the day of his patron saint. The beach
in amber light, windswept, smooth like the palm of a child.
Last week a man on patrol had a leg blown off, a landmine under
a used tire. Glass splinters spread with copper scrap, centuries
to come before turning into sea glass, splinters becoming smooth,
water-worn edges rounded by salt, like his other sea glass pieces. Flint
to fire to water, he bent to retrieve something, a dog tag chain,
name filed off.

Razor fencing keeps out no tide, a helmet swims around a tank
turret, blown-up armored trucks in prayer formation under dust shrouds,
steel cages made from their cabins. Sand clots around boot heels where
revenants now walk. A decapitated doll's head, witness to
their passage, and his, and later on, a hand-dug grave of a child.
A mania drew him forward through the saline that washed the
earth's wounds, deposit of new casualties. Like stones tumbled
in a barrel, objects defined and definite, polished featureless
surfaces. A camp flooded in scheduled cleansings, and
shelter offered in a concrete pillbox, one where German sailors
had taken poison.

There were other beaches, affinities of sand, other collectors—
of mortar shells, spare engine parts, military canteens—none
more serious in intent than the sea glass collector. The colors: Kelly
green for tenderness, brown for courage, white for peace,
amber for blood, teal blue for health. Once there was
black, ancient glass smelted with iron slag, for the empty space
below the heart. That one he inscribed with your Celan poem:
'The *shofar* place deep in the flowing text-voids at torch height
in the timehole: hear deep in with your mouth.'

You, dear reader, will remember his obsession as you again
read the words.

CINDERS

It began outside Krakow with an explosion near the Vistula,
then cramped ice floes. Though you smoked only a
cigarette or two a day, it was to burn to ashes. From impoverished
cafes, stripped of wrought iron, foreign ashtrays were
filched, Pernod and Dubonnet, chipped ceramic trefoils,
white with adjectives, barricades on the tables. Filched in your
bag, you started a collection more useful than books, less
useful than vodka. Icicles from roofs, thin crafted darts,
surprise the few children as they crash. The mottled call
of the ragspicker in counterpoint to chimes of Wawel
Cathedral, as a group of Hasidim walk under fur hats
(*shtreimel*).

You walked also, on your way to the salt mine, a safe
place after skirting the police barrier, 'sensations, frost-spindled'
as you imagine the long line once divided, the
shorter of the two with young and able-bodied. There was no
zweifelt, no between.

Now it is all about papers in order. There in the ghetto
is the house of a great-uncle who was killed, your
grandmother's brother a block from the *shule* 'where
he prayed every day.' A sign now says that Simchas
Torah is Saturday, opening anew the book of life,
'cold start—with hemoglobin.' Mongrels circle
each other outside a butcher shop outside of which bones
will be thrown. A raw wind ratchets up, the sun
had its dogs in the morning, a young girl plays hopscotch
on the sidewalk. When you passed her earlier, she
had been feeding a headless doll clumps of snow, letting
them drop into the hollow torso. There are winter
thoughts of renewal. The Vistula flows without
interruption, as do all things on this earth.

THE LINGUIST

The first word was one stolen: *gnomon*. Its meaning was
a guess, its sound wove a spell. It was not to assemble
a dictionary that you began a list. It was a reason you
couldn't have given then—reparations. There was a ventriloquism,
another who spoke them in your voice. You would
hear. Others followed. *Kitesilk. Grisaille. Lamia.*
You kept them in a small moleskin notebook. Once
by the lake, as you read aloud, you stared down the
open mouth of a frog and felt sterile thunder in the abyss.
Then you saw how 'a brightness sickles as though
words were gasping.' Watching, dreaming, *heimlos*,
you felt deserted by your guardian spirit, your *daimon*.

After that, single syllables were inconsolable. *Daub.*
Yawl. Schist. Each marked a leaves-taking in whose
wake you sank, a ballast shifting that had drowned
the vessel. You would know the end before beginning.
Glint. Words jumped in ambush, the remorse of sense,
an arrival of what was not invoked. They taught by
surprise like collateral damage, gratuitous pain.

They taught nothing cannot be felt,
nothing not freed from irrevocable dying. You
wrote them on scraps—paper or not—on a dog tag worn
around your neck, a talisman. *Mangle. Palings.*

You feel they are living, like fire, their incandescence
burns up all ungodliness. They gaze on you pleading,
you acknowledge their call. Why? you ask. The dead
don't know who they are, day and night are impassable,
unborn. They round in the wind's throat, the
wolf's howl. You listen: nothing. You look: a flash
of black fire on white.

They have weight. Gravity pulls. Gutturals are heavy,
sibilants are mealy, ready to flit away. Labiles rise and fall
with the tides, floundering in the neap. Under the
canopy of stars, according to lore, they decompose,
become unborn faces, shells of snails, the luff and the
leech, to convey the tattered revenant home.

Now the collection is lost. The words have decamped.
What is left but mute happenings? Their silent cry of
absence, their ill-reason.

HANGER OF CARPETS

A rug hangs, tassels knotted each by hand,
tribal signatures for reading an events calendar,
sacred markings rewritten as banalities,
how many carpets, rolled into cylinders,
spread double, triple over parquet,
once served other lives, lived in other homes,
lost earrings, locket of a wife
transported to Kaiserwald or Dachau,
a child's cutout doll, mementoes kept
not under an attic's loose floorboard,
but unremembered, 'the place is not nameable.'

No dates stamped on the underside's manifests,
bills of lading, *ketubot*, death certificates
faked so that bounty hunters can't trace you, no one searches
except a faint voice within, from the ruins
of a kitchen, in a camp sanitized
for 'inspection' where one whose head you held
in a dream, strands of whose pure white hair left
a crease on your palm as you recited
the Kaddish, below the breath so no one
could overhear. In the evening, guttering *yahrzeits*
upset starlings in the eaves that raucously
caw your name, or anyone's, to report,
to be there, to answer for an invented infraction or
infidelity, where any misdemeanor meant life
forfeited, maimed, an arm yanked from its socket,

to dig in the dark burial field, at dawn,
a poor grave for the saint whose name-day
was hidden ages ago in the cargo ship
on which your father, yourself, would have

arrived, disembarking in a new world, a new mind
to 'trust the trail of tears and learn to live.'

Come, unroll the carpets for an other welcome,
birth by fire, your second birth, that they proclaim.

SHIPWRECKS

In fog, in hoarfrost
a boat a revenant
without rudder
looks from the half-deck
with empty eye sockets
to watch the blizzard
a mother's cloak snapping
at the wind
the girl on the cot
beside the phantom apples
is aware of not feeling
cold in her hands

others sing 'Apples and Pears'
with a jump rope tied to
the main mast rigging
when a high pitched cry
assails a drinking glass
on the night table
until it shatters in sympathy
to a hundred splinters
coruscating
unmixed white light.
Inscribes a name
she was called
before she was born.

THE ISLAND

How it would be, off-island
the cumulus sinking toward the archipelago
like a plane's single-engine
stuttering with little altitude to spare
near Cliffside above the decayed
ruin of the Ashburton

ancient sailors wheel by minute after minute
nobody whom you knew in life
nobody who could lift the stone
that blocks the cave mouth to the sea

you have gone under
to try to come back
as one *disappeared*, a dark awakening
the way the dead carry on
not knowing that destiny waits,
a run-on past buried in the flux
of your indulgence, confused
desire, the child's you once were

fabricating another ending
subject to tides and trials
expelled gracelessly seaward
your unlived lives trail in a wake of plastic
fleeing this prison, its moat
of an ocean—Okeanos—that spawns
monsters to devour ships in fleet
bearing names of refugees who
once crossed to where they wished
to have landed,

each dog tag you place back in lapsed time
each eulogy said in trance of mind
its must of shipwrecks and uncharted
founderings lets you speak a voice
free from learned confusion that would
emphatically deny the right to be just.

SIMCHAS TORAH

The line you once copied was lost. I kept it in
a stack, it was Greek, about betrayal, but I
could not say who wrote it. It concerned
a truce that was duplicitous, the sun—a flower
of light—was in it, fruit of figs, a street in a
conquered city ravaged in a long siege. The
man there was a collector of things, a packrat
more intent on gathering and keeping than
seeing inhumanity in the world. Who was
inconsequential enough to see him? In the poem,
aware of war, he nonetheless walks on barricades
as a demon, hungry for human feeling. An
earlier version had him figure in a dream who
died among traitors. In another he is hero in
a firebombing and from a synagogue rescues
the book inscribing names of the living for
the year to come. As he reads, he finds his own
family nowhere on the list. There is coded
writing on the leather cover in script thought to be
Macedonian. Given the task to translate, he
comes up with the missing line. You gave me it:
'and it is innocent, as it must remain.' It belongs
to the city, like the salamanders that scramble up
stone walls, to catch sight of them, you must first look.

CAMBODIA

The mountain was a giant Buddha
carved under rays of a young sun.

Pray you there, though if the just aren't in
need of prayer, leave fruit and flowers instead.

While the bus had driven through the night,
we passed around a single canteen of water.

Air travel was cancelled for reasons of which flares
on foothills east remind us: insurrection.

A smashed-in moon as the jungle ventriloquizes
mortars popping, lightning flashes.

Across an open journal in the slant of a
flashlight beam, you read 'against every barb
in the wire.'

The soldiers are bored at the check-point,
gray-beards hunched with the brutishness
of their job.

Our papers confuse them, does it matter
if we are not their enemy's friends?

Monkeys scream at a helicopter above,
then the silence of their making escape.

Guards fire in blankness of fear, strange
how a soul, loosened, provokes renunciation
before it is cast again into star-filled nebulae.

Luna moths float in the headlights, almost
translucent, engine heat rises like incense to heaven,
curdling the light rays.

You empty a bag of dry rose petals
bought on market day in Phnom Penh. They
find their way to earth, reluctant to give up
loft in the time it takes to fall to gravity.

COMING HOME

To return is to not leave
gray walls that contain no trace
of you or of any other
who would dare speak your name
in the obverse of babble
retelling a dream that flowers above you
with petals like an agave's trumpet,
mute in summons from the flower
of many voices

one a dread silencing the waves
one a birth-rung to light
interwoven like roots in stone

while a gale shakes them free
into oxygen that purifies as it kills
now you who must tell where you stay
if you are to be found

if not in particles that contrail west and fade
in the red of a sun's warning
if not in the body risen
above scrum clouds of day's dying.

if not

THE ESCAPEE

The order to keep still on the dank bed
of loam, the killing fields of marmots and fishers
their musk heavy, cloyingly sweet, food
of microbes able to distill perfume from death.

Sleep refused us, the moon a well-sharpened blade
left off its shadowing, a woman who fed birds
ceased to scatter crumbs, wandering pit to pit in search
of scrap, and became a footfall whose singleness
froze blood in our veins. Nighthawks' shrieks
syncopated with the sputter-spray of artillery
flares bouncing above tree tops to bring sight to
pages of your journal, script running over
onto the ferns in which young girls in school uniforms
played, a singsong mixing with rope
salvaged from a munitions dump by the marsh,
their handless bodies in white shifts, carefree in movement,
unlike you, stiff with your preoccupations with mines
and the intricacy of ordnance work.

Bats zigzagged over mulberry trees, stirring
them like barrage balloons in the spirit of our bivouac.
Was there no ambush or tripwire, no pent-up breath,
no petrol or gunpowder smell, no body lifeless on the
camber that we walked, safe passage to the monk's cell?

What you had said about tufts of wool speared on
bramble, a dog whining by the gutted chassis of a
bus, a corner of a torn passport photo, could not be
heard by the heart in my mouth. There on tarmac,
the drumbeat of blood in the temples, at each step,
an article given, moly to counteract fear

for which those astride their own grave
would be forgiven, life sentences commuted in the firefight
while for you, as you slip aside, 'a tear rolls
back into its eye.'

The physics of bereavement.

THE MISSING PERSON

A collection of fruit flies conjures a mirage over
a bowl of mangoes, an image like that of the shroud,
almost not there, insisting on its absence.

I think of you, drafted into an army of machetes,
using yours to peel skin sliding from the blade—

mine, a small pen knife to pare my fingernails.
Your notebook and photograph I would have
thrown on the fire

to incinerate those raw mornings in Munich, a
squadron of school children by your park bench,

the innocence of time unrecorded, repaired
in poems you wrote there 'it is the spirit of
unexpressed and eternally living savagery.'

Sirens sound during your vigil, their alarm
passed into a maze, clouds reflected from a broad lake

eye like a hawk's from an updraft, motionless at noon.
There were no shadows, the police too

bestial for light or dark to witness kindness

no remains though we search morgues for days on end
as if your suffering had been erased by
earth's goodness.

I listened to wind parsing the marsh grass
a thin piping that brought back your whistle

blowing a blade from a leafy weed, its pitch rising
above garlic fields, a copse of linden, the
haze of stardust

to a pure space, a journey you would make again
now later gathered before us as we read words
you left, that keep the secret you hid

of how a life must try to seize its radiance
while it can.

NACHLASS

There are no rivers on the island.
Deep quarries, yes, and Eel Creek, navigable in
surfeit of winter rain, otherwise a wet footprint.

Winds from mustard fields airbrush yellow
pollen onto sleeping corn cribs, a cawing flock
from the churchyard remembers hope isn't
an advance on mortal life. One grave dug before white
weather, its soil marbled with chalk and marl,
wetted down for a lobsterman who overstayed
the tide. Inside, logs of shipwrecks, manifests
of lading, a registry of arrival written on
parchment, ledger of birth records that noted the years
ahead to be lived.

We came with longing, left as stale as cemetery
prayers *sotto voce,* sober, deep in
voice, as rain washes copper spouts. Drops race down the
hand-blown glass of the refectory, dimming
sight, you say *as if without us we could be we.*

Ferns beside the doorway, pallid under frost,
above a stoup almost dry from matins. Mirrored
by its surface, you see your eyes and behind,
where you dreamed yourself into your life's
desire, and fleetingly where it will end. It is
in place of asylum, minus an orison, a hallelujah
played by fingers on a mock keyboard.

Such sadness scours memory, time bears
still-born moments, a breach birth entangled
in its own umbilicus.

Alone, your mother away, you hold your father's
urn on which I have written his Hebrew name
in your own hand while you stand upright in praise
of the words. The hours are suspended between the letters
while stars wait eternally *there*, watchful for
absence, watching absence, and leave no earthly mark
for the Hunter who watches, head bowed, to the west.

Death, where is your script? you ask, whispering
for finality in my ear. Above, night
spreads open its vault to let a brace of cranes pass,
in the dream of writing.

There you wake to your unending pause, to look
for the work, the name of _____.

CLASHING ROCKS

From a giant fist, a handful of islands thrown
southward, an immobile armada that seeks largesse and
leaves beneath it a fleet of hulls, to join earlier unmanned
rigs in wait to wreck survivors, by winter
ice gnashing prows, ballast freed to drop to a salt crypt.

You who knew how spare the sheath of life
was beside the sea, plenum of death, hungry to
undo the knowing

an alliance of the two in which the waking dark was
forgotten in your striving to remain, to dwell in
uncertainty on this turret of rock, granted trial
in mist and hail, irrevocable as salt that
suffers in its healing

you also knew cries of sailors, lost as they
are to the earth, that blend with songs of whales

the deep-bellied call evokes a night sky, astral
space blinks without interest as it looks past the
rock-strewn archipelago

to take measure of a human pulse, its throb under
and through the heart, susceptible to mindings
of fate as you have felt

from the very first cry, suctioned clear of sea-
salt fluid from where you came and have
come back, time and again

the plaintive cries of a small child lost in a seizure
of recognition, who lives confusion, alone
in a trance

beginning again to remember the pain as
return, and return to folds of hope, to a
source seen but for when you look away

as you do in the face of this small beginning.

MOUNT FUJI

You with hot tea rested at the sixth station,
a heavy moisture weighting flaps of the tent, drops
that condense, fall at random tempos onto
stone piles, our funerary trek slowed by a
mountaintop storm. The smell of scorched
wool and red-hot iron for branding walk sticks,
mumbled prayers of pilgrims, first aid for a
gashed foot of an elder nun.

Talk in countless dialects of the crater, shrouded
pathways to it, the impossible meteor streak near midnight.
The path is hung like a gallery with wrinkled glossy black
and whites from *Life* of a royal ascent. Along
it, a different past in cairns, cenotaphs, wedgestones,
prayers on rags knotted to trees, illegible
petitions of longing felt too deeply to ask.

I made a small pile of stones beside you
before lifting the urn for the next climb. Under
one rock, a fissure holds a nest of baby mice.
A Japanese farmer had us pose for a photograph,
holding the Rising Sun (*Kyoku-jitsu-ki*)
as a wind threatened to steal it.

The dark was a velvet curtain, its folds
protecting your spirit, but I shivered as the
ground trembled beneath our feet. Then I was
following the acrid breath of the next one ahead,
not asking why, remembering we who
came into the world were not asked to. One foot, then
a next, body obedient, under a sickle moon
cut in clouds.

Cry of some nocturnal raptor disturbed with its
quarry by ice crashing on the tundra. There were
five more stations, each with fire for branding, tea
for comfort, always a desire to sleep
to the sloughing gravel dropped into an abyss.

At the penultimate, a sudden flapping of wings but
when we looked down the precipice, there was
only your urn with us, no fallen sign, no remembrance
of how few had given more to others than you. The
peak was ablaze, a young sun having set fire to
the last teahouse blinding the dozen souls
gathered there for morning exercises.

The flames let steam vent, hovering before it
tilted east and vanished above pennants. You
could be a dust particle in flight—thin air
purified of the filth of war by primordial light
not yet gathered to petty purpose. Morning damp
clinging to our hair, as the flaps flare, pollen
and moth wreathed us, and then, the cap removed,
ash flew up, as your essence like an overtone
searched for a next station higher up.

THE WHALE'S HARMONY

Sheer basalt above Dark Harbor
a cubist cityscape in flames at sunset
we dangle our legs over the clashing rocks
feeling vertigo of heroes while below, kelp at sea
mimics the syncopation of swimmers
caught in a rip tide, puffins and auks
bend wings against a front that races in.

Even at our height air is salt-sweetened
while harbor seals lie rotting on dulse
that will be sundried for sale to tourists.
A colony of stone fisher shacks lines the strand
now deserted, boats lashed to the upland side
shutters nailed tight with driftwood spikes.
The cliff seems to rise and fall with nervous cries
of great sea birds that patrol the expressionless face
before seeking shelter among tar pines inland.

The same wind that sings across bottle-mouthed caves
stings our ears until we have to clap our palms
over them, crying out in pain.
White is its color, coordinating waves with sand.

The only exception, a great wrought iron
scalding pot, inverted, under which we stored
empty nets, bait boxes, metal cases of motor oil.
A platoon of lobster traps has been blown free
and blocks a steep grade to the landing.
We abandon the rim, our safety, and walk the road
strewn with pine needles, tufts of rocket, unbraided rope
strands, shells of tiny crabs, barely born.
Far off in brackish water below, a humpback

breaches, then a double roll before sounding the calm
depths.

They say it is for the whale that the sea provides, driving
krill to shore. I see him at night, fathoms below
an immemorial ocean, to become scripture of the event

to engrave origin in the denial of mind.

THE LIGHTHOUSE

Across the bay, light that never sleeps,
a surface shimmers beneath imagined boats
disregarding admonitions of the fog horn
against torpedoes from the harbor installation.
On mornings by a heliport near the lighthouse,
I can see men lift nets too thick with herring
for a single ship's hold, to be hauled back for smoking.
By the shacks, white skeletons of spruce
eaten by a fungus blight from Asia
stand vigil around an anti-aircraft battery.
In the past they shielded the village from
a north wind that sought misery,
bats presently find refuge in their hollows
before dropping into air to forage insects.
Villagers say they too will be gone
once the bay is fished out. In place of
a plaintive screech of hunger, silence will
thicken and be spoken.

THE MUSICIAN

A campfire little more than embers
dry kindling burns toward a common center

in woods as thick as clumped fur
frost could not find a path to chill a body

on a whittled stick you mime a Bach fugue
its notes drawing away the air between us
suctioning it to a vacuum

your fingers poised over invisible stops
mounting, and beyond, chords of light—

for the soldier in Benares who left
his prayer rug by the burning *gahts*

for the rosary in the gutter at Lourdes
for the pebble on the stone lantern in Gaza

to stay the ghost from following you
for the painkillers forgotten in Paris
in haste to evacuate

for the Vespa in Milan that jammed a gear
before a dud grenade landed at your feet

for the coat of moonlight in whose radiance
they will find peace as your remembrance.

BEFOREHAND

Two purple finches pared
a hemlock of larvae
in a minute, a second time
in the garden after sixty years
a *déjà vu* of where my father dug
between roots and stones
for potato plants
in neat string-lined rows
heirloom tomatoes
curled over Army surplus wire—
Tante Faiga's idea—
shaded by a hickory tree
under which my mother
labored in a window past
through three pregnancies
her body fecund
yielding yearly harvests
along with bumper crops of pig-nuts
the vision now bursting upon me
that there were precious
few vegetables for our table.

MATINS

In the night letter box, your calling—mail
delivery—rewrites forgetfulness onto each
address line, misspelling by accident,
mislaying on purpose, by weakness of will, though
yours remains firm. Names of addressees smudged,
blotted, annotated, inverted (deliberately), or
missing altogether so that arrival, contingent
on good intent, is given to chance. You must confess
to the censor's blade, redactions of the heart,
conspiracies of thought, betrayals to which each postage
stamp bears witness, bills of mortality cut
short, overruns at expiration, lost valedictions,
words with meanings excised, and accept how sentences
rise as ash from the postmaster's Warm Morning,
to leave residues of infidelity, contumely, and war,
the fire's plume fatally pierced by artillery tracers
from the mortars beyond the beachhead.

You mustn't withhold manifests, Trieste, Cyprus, Malta,
Thessalonica, or papers of passage,
identity papers, work papers, health records,
charts of lineage and descent, ledgers of
deposit and transfer, ancestral claims,
church affiliations, bills of lading, tax bills,
or disputes of credit. Handwriting cramped, to speak
to the dread of naked, unopened misgivings.
Speak to the first slit, throat exposed, onionskin page
crispated from sea water, inner pages tendering
ration coupons, promotion forms, jury summonses,
will and testaments, newspaper clippings of
warships, blank scraps with thumbprints in blood.

In a locked red metal box with a handle
(still unopened), where your boyhood
stamp collection is stored, letters would
whisper praise for sealing the
postage, to lips and tongue of the sender, her
fingertips tacky from inserting within folds her
prayer for his safe arrival. They speak the old
language, an oral history of lost and found and
irreparably gone, as well as prophecy of what will be newly
born, added and deleted, all that blesses
the work of fortune—the aleatory moment.

In letters rife with knowing the slug in the coin slot, nail
in the tire, quack remedy, wrong car key, mis-
attributed name, or uncrossed 't', how news can end
in the wrong box. In a waking
dream of the post office fire, its sorting bins
flitting with infernal flames, a whirlwind raising
reward posters to white heat, excise stamps,
return-to-sender stamps. postage due stamps, no-
such-address stamps—blasts apart the single un-
latched casement window, incinerates it, and escapes
into a pure starless night.

There in sidereal space, as unignited carbon dust, war letters
from your father, Okinawa, Guam, Midlands,
Philippines, Iwo Jima, words of untenable pain,
of love, of longing for your mother, adoration of
the angel informing the globe of cells that
would house your infant soul.

These letters of loss and repair testify to how you became
a collector of lapsed time.

ACKNOWLEDGEMENTS

Without the support of my wife, Kate Hamilton, the
inspiration behind this work would have been lacking.
Without the encouragement and linguistic expertise of
Todd Swift, publisher of Black Spring Press Group, the book
would not have been possible. Thanks also to the dedicated
staff of the press, especially Amira, Cate and Edwin.